Coloring the Past:
1860s

MAUREEN TAYLOR

WWW.MAUREENTAYLOR.COM

Picture Perfect Press

COLORING THE PAST
1860s

Copyright © 2015

by

Maureen Taylor
www.maureentaylor.com

All rights reserved. Reproduction or utilization of this work in any form, by any means now known or herein after invented, including but not limited to xerography, photocopying and recording, and in any storage and retrieval system, is forbidden without permission from the copyrighted holder.

Introduction

Apple green, orange and cinnamon pink aren't colors you usually associate with the clothing worn by people in old photos. Gray, black and white are what we see when we look those old pictures so it's easy to jump to a conclusion about how boring ancestral clothing was by viewing it in a photograph. That's far from the reality. A Victorian woman wouldn't have been caught dead in the washed out versions of their dresses visible in nineteenth century pictures.

Bright colors and subtle shaded fabrics were available but different colors appear dark or light in images. Below is a newspaper quote that explains the problem of viewing colors in old photos, advising women on choosing their clothing colors carefully for portraits and addressing how it looks when photographed. The author also added general tips on how women could accent their appearance based on complexion and hair. The details in this article gives us hints about what colors our ancestors liked and wore as well as what they looked like in images.

HOW TO DRESS FOR A PHOTOGRAPH (EXCERPT)

Let me offer a few words of advice touching dress. Orange color for certain optical reasons is photographically, black; blue is white; other shades or tone of color are proportionally darker or ligher [sic] as they contain more or less of these colors. The progressive scale of photographic color commences with the highest. The others stand thus: white, light, blue, violet, pink, mauve, dark blue, lemon, blue-green, leather brown, drab, cerise, Magenta, yellow green, dark brown, purple, red, amber, moroon [sic], orange, dead black. Complexion has to be much considered in connection with dress. Blondes can wear much lighter colors than brunettes. The latter always present better pictures in dark dresses, but neither look well in positive white. Violent contrasts of color should be especially guarded against. [1]

---

[1] "How to dress for a photograph." *New Orleans Times*, April 9, 1865, 2.

FASHIONS IN FULL COLOR

Beginning in the 1840s, photographers employed artists to tint and colorize their images from pink cheeks to full outfits. Every month, women read through fashion magazines to see the latest styles *and* colors. *Godey's Lady's Book* (1830-1898) featured hand colored fashion plates in the front of every issue. A woman could then take these plates depicting Americanized Paris fashions to their dressmaker or milliner to participate in the design of their clothing by selecting different fabrics, colors or by mixing elements from several different fashion plates. Thankfully, period hand colored photographs and full color nineteenth century fashion plates let us peek into their closets. A virtual rainbow of shades could be found in their wardrobes.

Popular colors for women in the 1860s were shades of brown, natural colors and even some bright shades. For instance, Italy's struggle for independence in the early 1860s made red a common color. The wide range of fabric colors also included: madder brown, dark chocolate, cocoa brown, cinnamon pink, bright reddish pinks, light aqua, turkey red, crimson, indigo, and pale peach.

The colors worn by women depended on their age and circumstances. Younger women tended toward bright shades while older women leaned toward darker colors, a fact that makes older women in photographs all look like they are wearing black garb.

A dark dress or suit doesn't mean a person is in mourning. Ebay descriptions often mention a "bride in mourning" but that's often not the case. Many Civil War brides wore purple out of respect for the troops, a color that would appear dark in a photo. In general women in mourning wore dead black (a fabric without sheen) but popular mourning colors were also gray, lavender, white, purple and mauve depending on the stage of mourning and their relationship to the deceased.

DYEING FABRICS

Until the late 1850s all fabric dyes were derived from natural sources, but in 1856 Englishman William Perkins was experimenting with quinine (an anti-malaria drug). His experiment failed, but he serendipitously discovered a synthetic purple, which became known as aniline purple and, later, mauve. Perkins patented his process and opened a dye works to produce the synthetic substance. Other non-organic dye was soon to become available. Brilliant pinks—magenta and solferino--named after Italian towns were widely used.

Colored patterned fabrics were also available. Stripes were used for walking dresses. Tattersall fabric, a checked patterned, was available in browns and tan. Also common were alpaca fleece dresses (derived from llamas) with contrasting decorative elements; dark on light and white on black.

The next time you look at a historical photo, close your eyes and try substituting colors. Remember our ancestors were fashion conscious creatures the same as us.

COLORING THE PAST

I've collected hand colored photographs and fashion plates to use in my work as The Photo Detective to assist with photo identification and interpretation. Lecture audiences often ask about ancestral fashion choices. The popularity of adult coloring pages gave me an idea: "Why not create a set that would help users "see" the past in full color?"

PLATES

These pages, taken from actual nineteenth century sources in my collection, give you an opportunity to colorize the 1860s in authentic shades. Try your hand at coloring the scenes from everyday life in the 1860s, women's bonnets and fashions worn by everyone in the family. There are 25 plates in this packet.

When you're done, you'll never look at your photographs the same way.

COLORING SUGGESTIONS

- I've left the specific color description out on purpose <smile>. Use your imagination and think about your favorite colors.
- Shade or blend pencil to obtain varying results.
- Practice with your pencils on a separate sheet of paper first so that you understand how the lead in your set of pencils looks shaded or full color. Every pencil manufacturer's lead is different.
- I'll offer other color suggestions in the Facebook group, "Coloring the Past."

Pencils

These suggested 8 pencil colors were matched as close as possible to the colors used in those original fashion plates. They are just the beginning. Use the standard black and white pencil in your existing coloring set.

Blick Studio Pencils	Prismacolor Colored Pencils
Azure Blue 22063-5911	True Blue PC903
Dark Ochre 22063-8211	Spanish Orange PC1003
Indigo Blue 22063-5201	Copenhagen Blue PC906
Pink 22063-3061	Rose PC928
Salmon Pink 22063-3511	Blush Pink PC928
Sap Green 22063-7091	Apple Green PC912
Vermillion 22063-3281	Pale Vermillion PC921
Violet 22063-6511	Violet PC932

Share YOUR RESULTS
I'd LOVE to see the finished sheets!

- Email me photos/scans of one of the plates you've colored so I can share them on social media
- #coloringthepast and post your completed plate on your social media account. Share the post with me by including the #photodetective.
- Post to the private Coloring the Past Facebook group.

About the Plates

Cover Image:
"Les Modes Parisiennes, July 1865

Peterson's Magazine, February 1861

Godey's Lady's Book, April 1866

1. Straw, trimmed with velvet and ostrich feather
2. Braided straw trimmed with flowers, pearl and silver ornaments
3. Same but with different trimmings
4. Glengary crown for a child
5. Derby trimmed with flowers, velvet and silver pendents.

Godey's Lady's Book, February 1864

"Hebe Dress" of poplin with velvet trim.

Godey's Lady's Book,
APRIL 1866

"Robe Dress" Zouave bordered jacket is in bright colors. Leghorn straw hat with ribbon and a feather.

Godey's Lady's Book,
OCTOBER 1860

"The Jeddo", a morning dress of silk. The bodice is trimmed to match the skirt.

Godey's Lady's Book,
JULY 1863

"Fancy Paletot, For the Country" of silk, mohair/silk braid.

Godey's Lady's Book,
1863

"A Robe Dress" of wool.

Godey's Lady's Book,
1867

"Spring Walking Costume" of silk and plaid shawl. Bonnet is silk, straw and lace.

Godey's Lady's Book,
1863

An Evening Dress of silk.

Godey's Lady's Book,
JANUARY 1867

"Skating Party"

Godey's Lady's Book,
1862

Silk on silk dress trimmed with velvet. Hat is trimmed with lace, violets and ribbons. 2w

Godey's Lady's Book,
AUGUST 1863

"The Adolphe Coat" of silk and velvet.

Godey's Lady's Book,
DECEMBER 1863

Godey's Lady's Book,
DECEMBER 1863

"Fancy Pen-Wiper" for a doll's head.

Godey's Lady's Book,
JANUARY 1862

"The Marine Jacket" of Poplin (dress and jacket)

Godey's Lady's Book,
SEPTEMBER 1865

1. Poplin, trimmed with ribbon
2. Poplin, trimmed with ribbon.
3. Pique, trimmed with mohair braid.
4. Wool cloth
5. Poplin shirt and velvet cap.

Godey's Lady's Book,
MARCH 1865

"The Ebro" no specific fabric mentioned.
Rich colors.

Godey's Lady's Book,
SEPTEMBER 1862

"Pique trimmed with braid"

Godey's Lady's Book
JULY 1862

"The Proposal"

Godey's Lady's Book
JULY 1862

"What O'Clock"

Godey's Lady's Book,
1862

Godey's Lady's Book,
1862

"Gored Dress, Trimmed en Zouave"

Godey's Lady's Book,
1862

"The Seville" Silk with roses, foliage and grapes.

Godey's Lady's Book
JANUARY 1862

"The Doubtful Note"

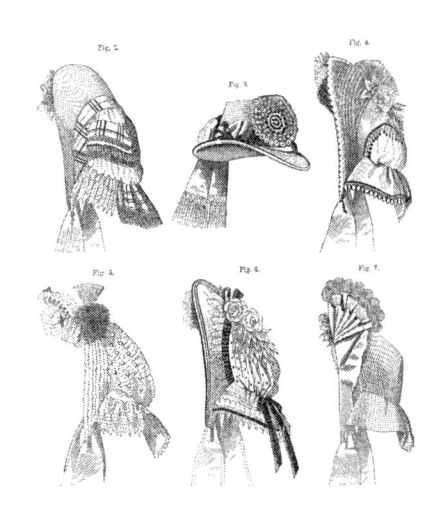

Godey's Lady's Book,
AUGUST 1863

1. Decorated with tulle, ribbon and chenille fringe.
2. Leghorn straw, ribbon, feathers and flowers. Trimmed with velvet.
3. Crinoline with tulle; crown trimmed with silk. Trim is velvet, jet, roses, grass and lace.
4. Dress bonnet of tulle, leaves, and lace.
5. Trimmed with spotted net, lace and velvet with roses.
6. Leghorn straw, trimmed with silk and ostrich feathers.

Godey's Lady's Book,
1862

Silk dress with Muslin Garibaldi style shirt. Boy's suit of poplin trimmed with velvet worn with straw hat trimmed with velvet and plume.

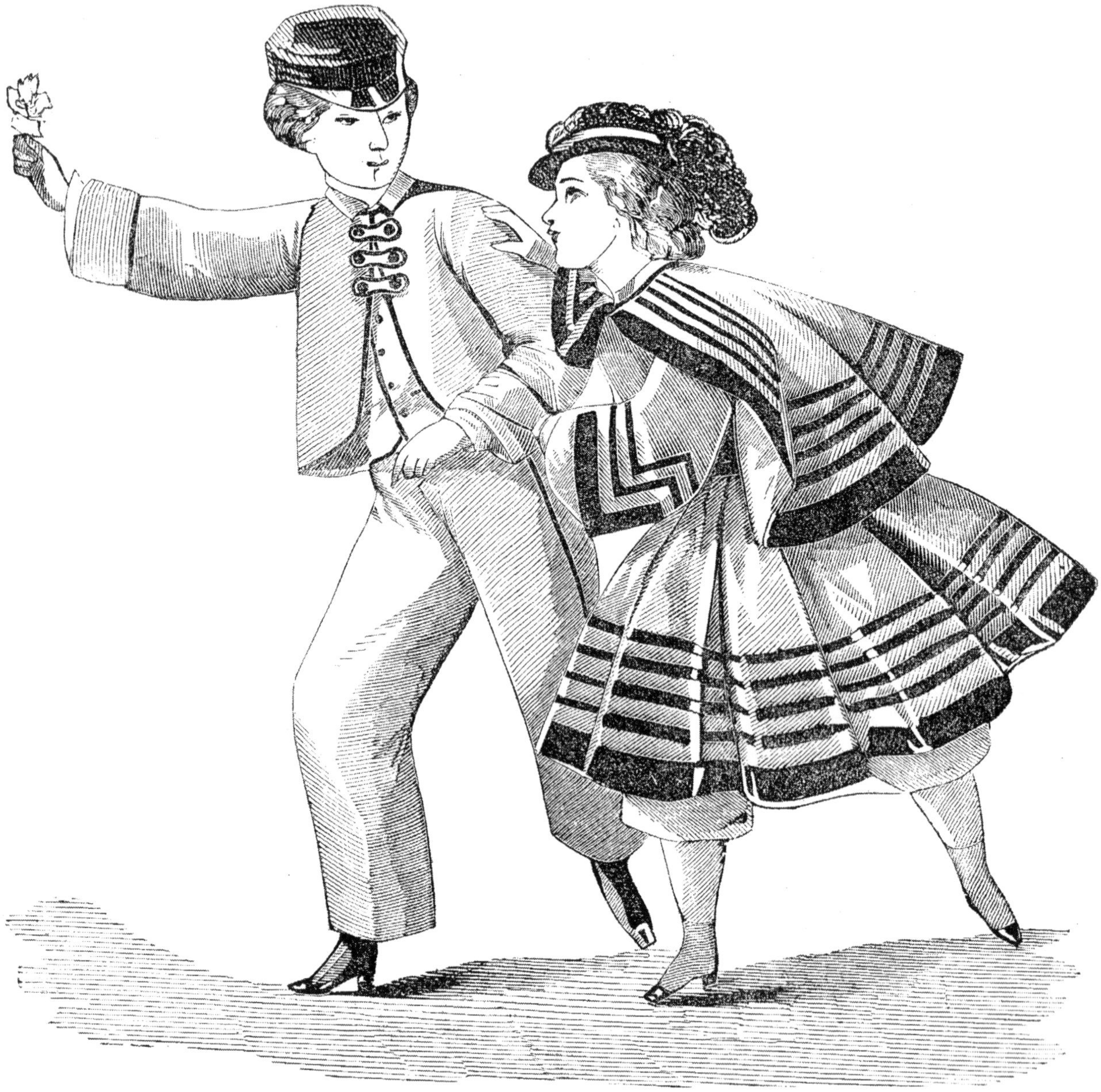

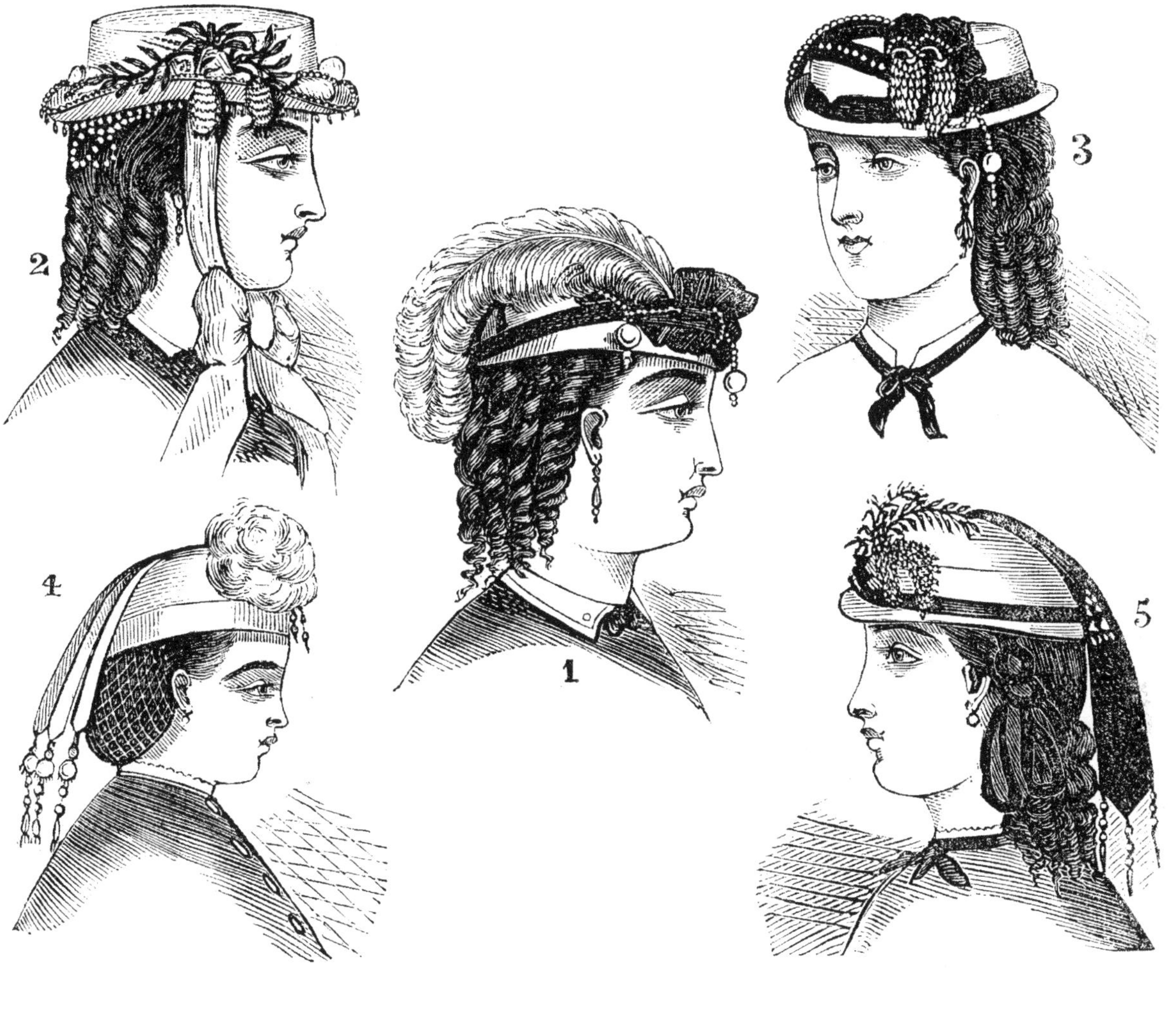
2
3
1
4
5

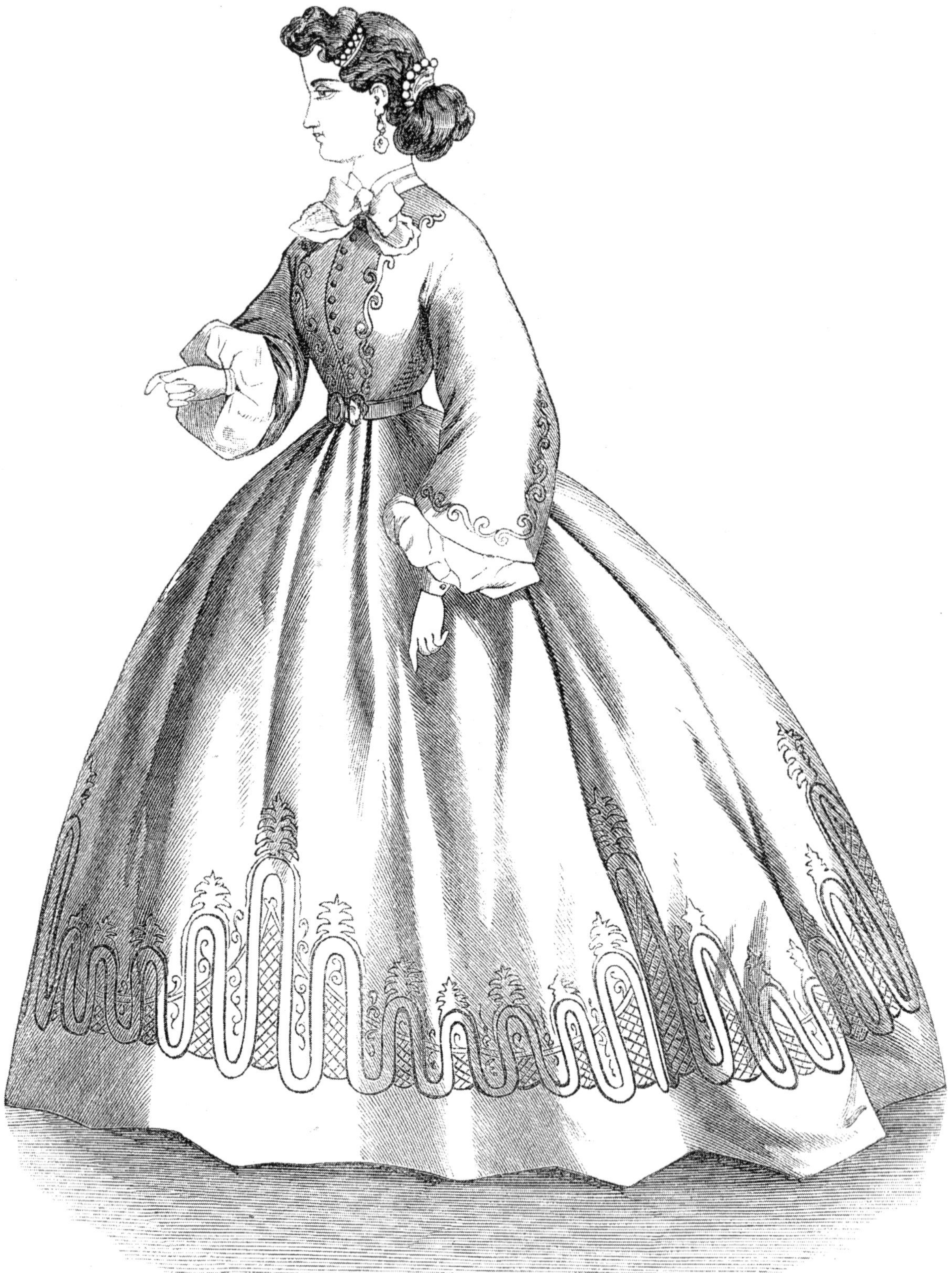

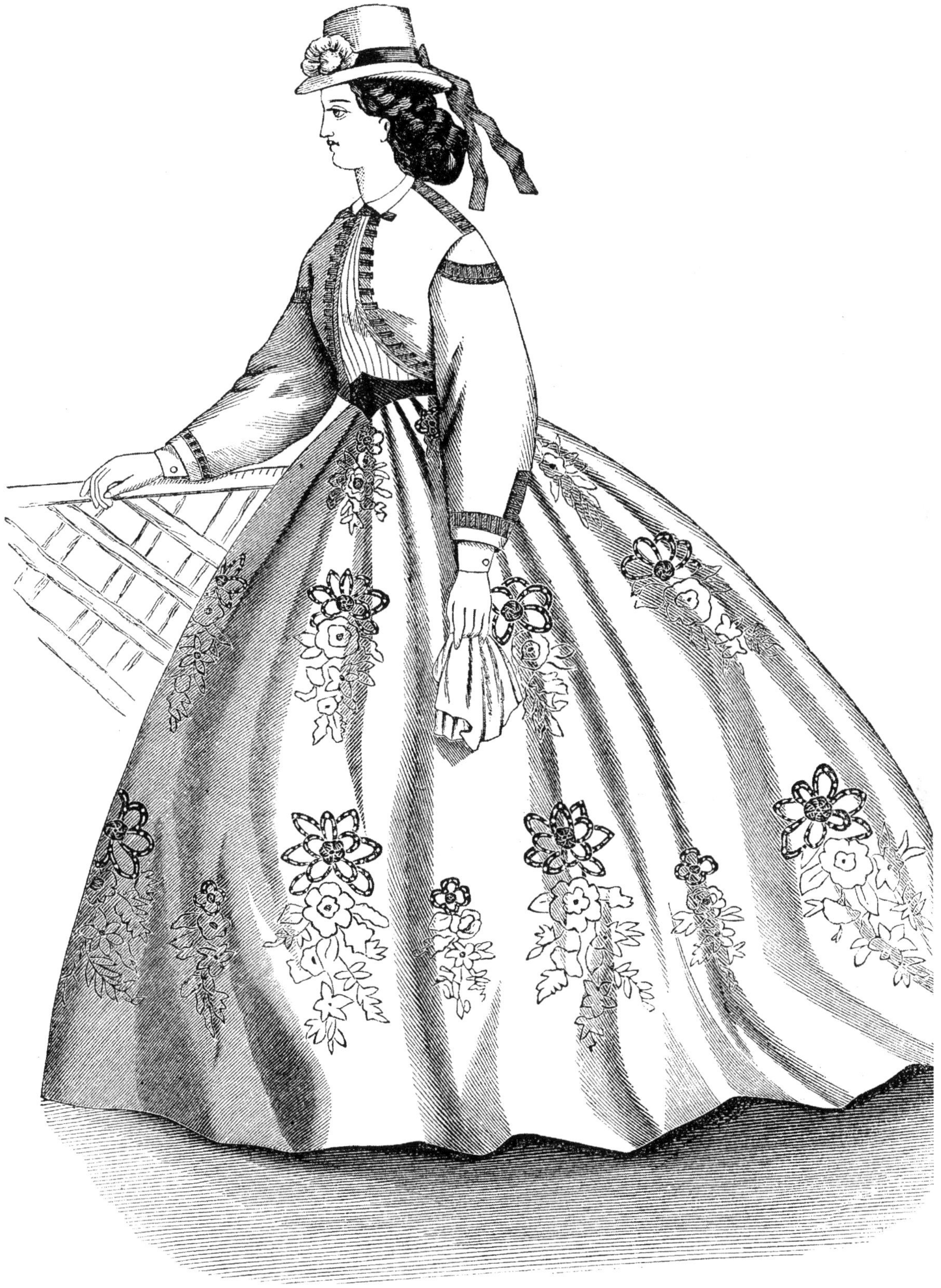

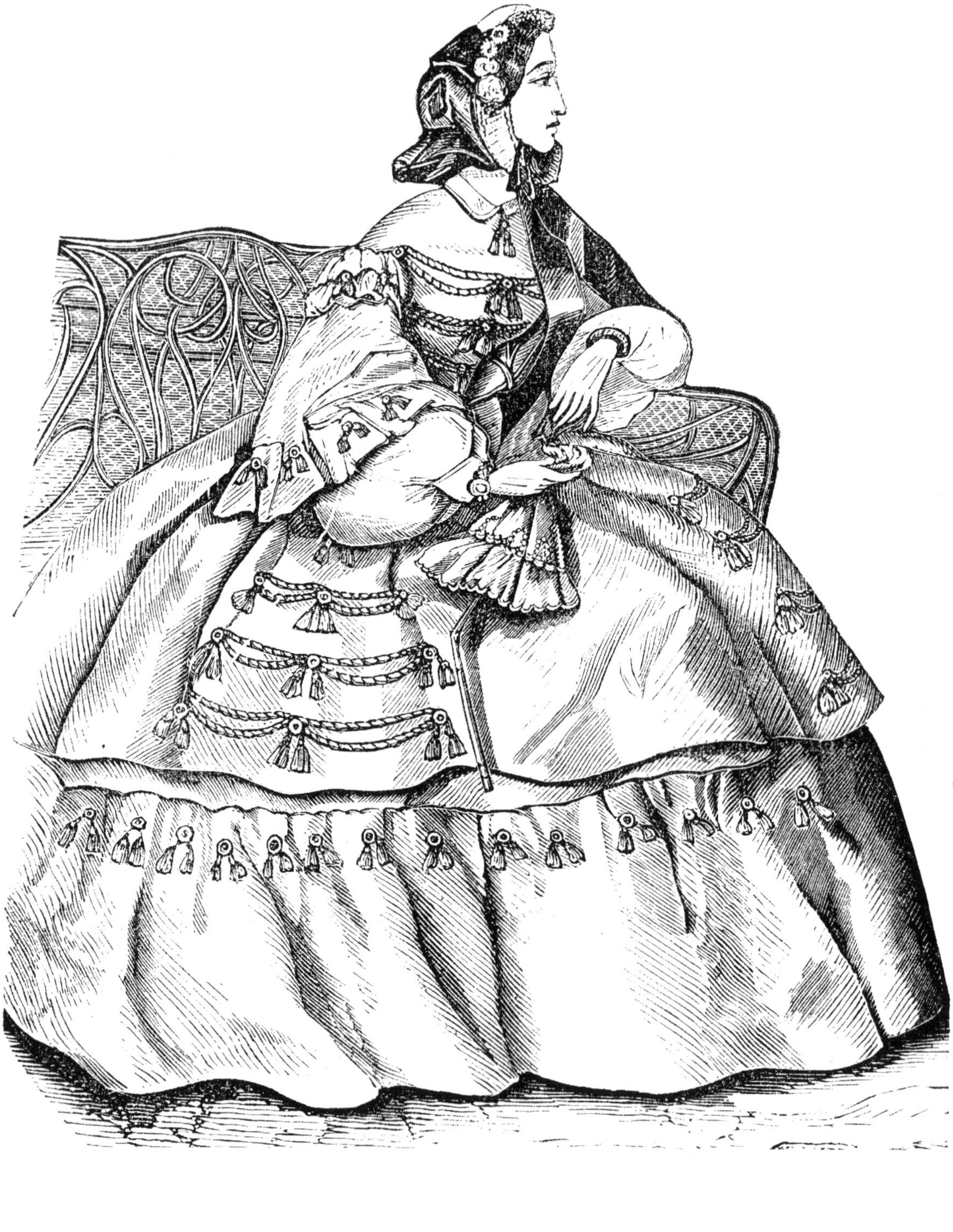

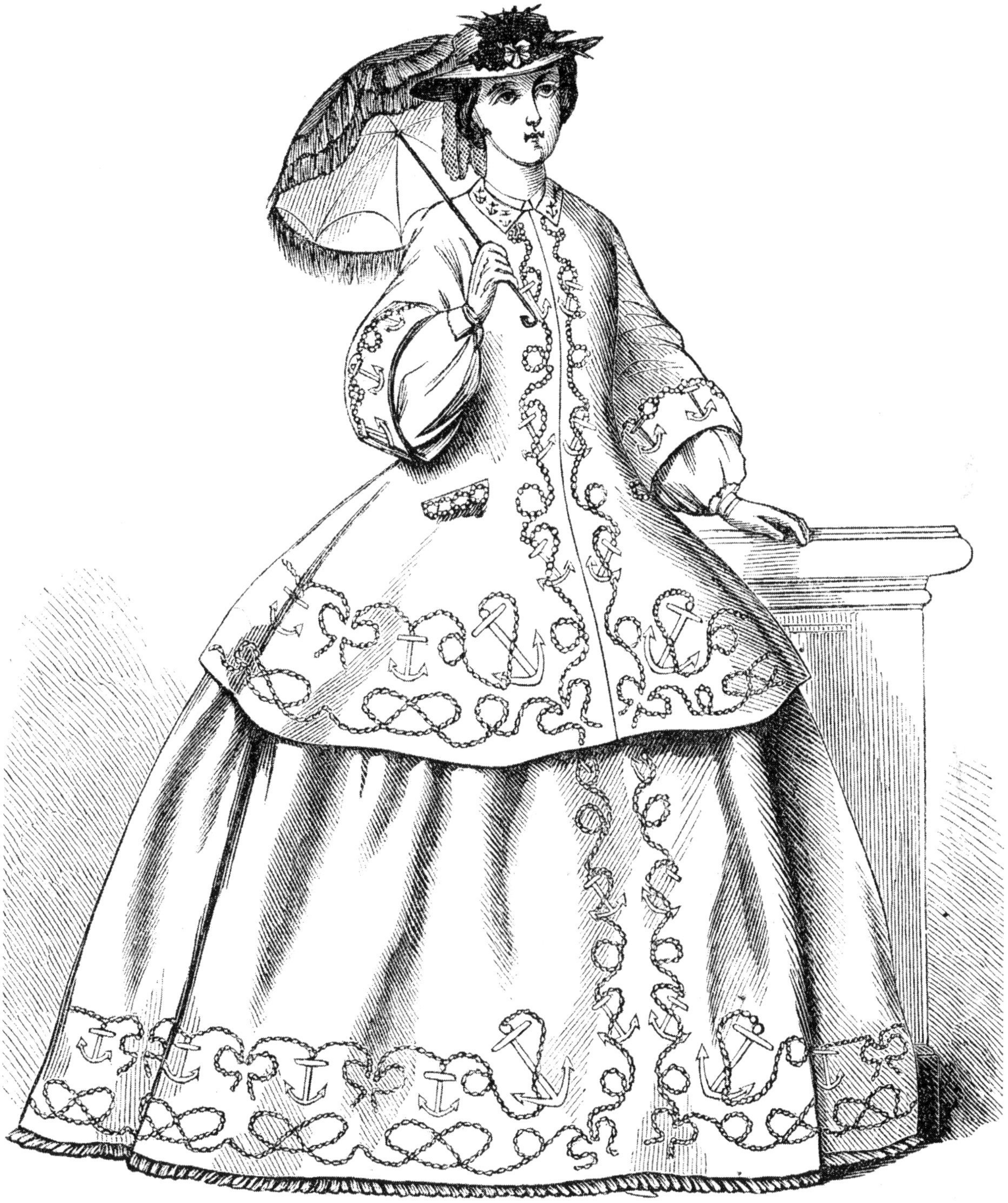

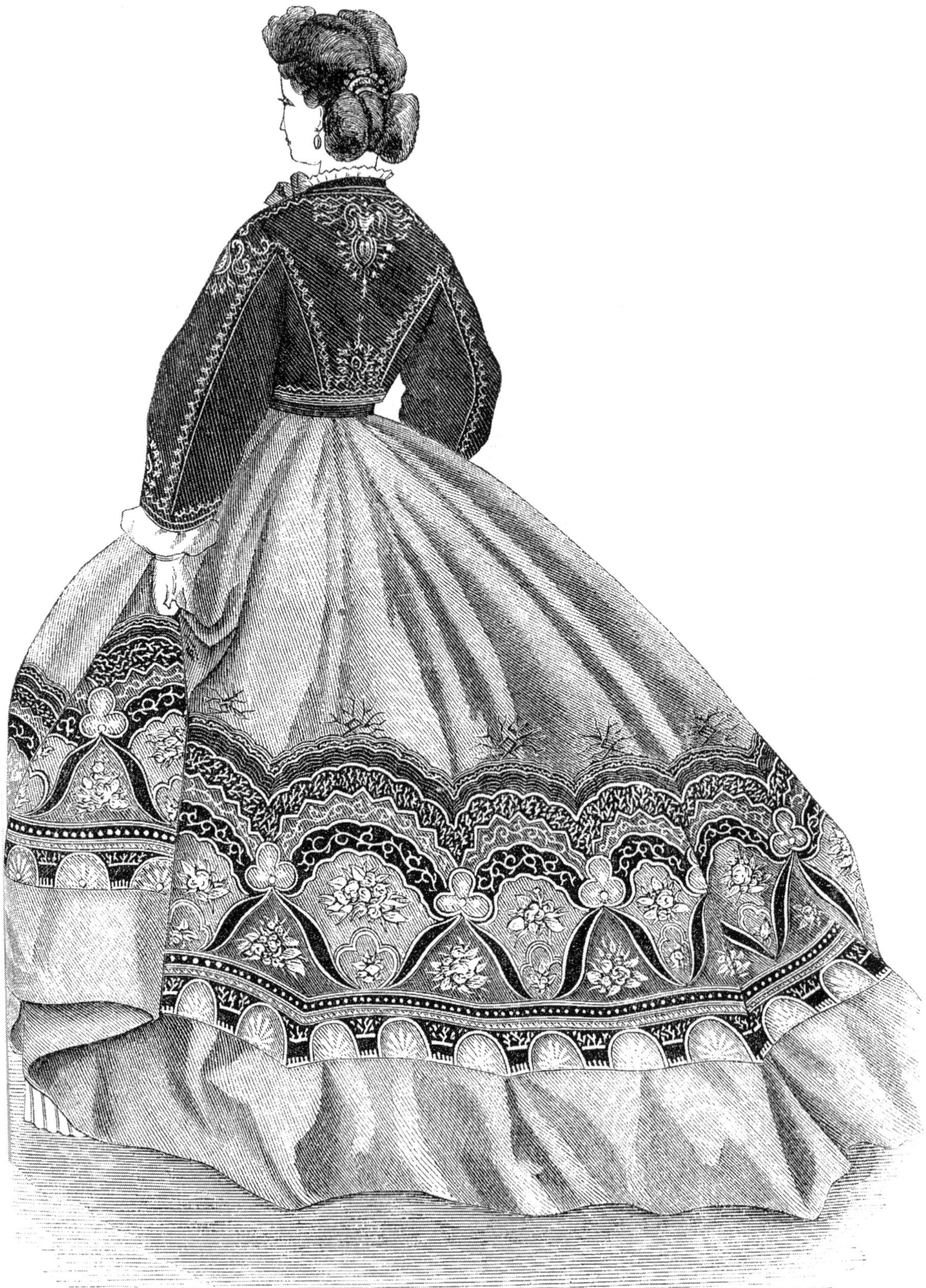

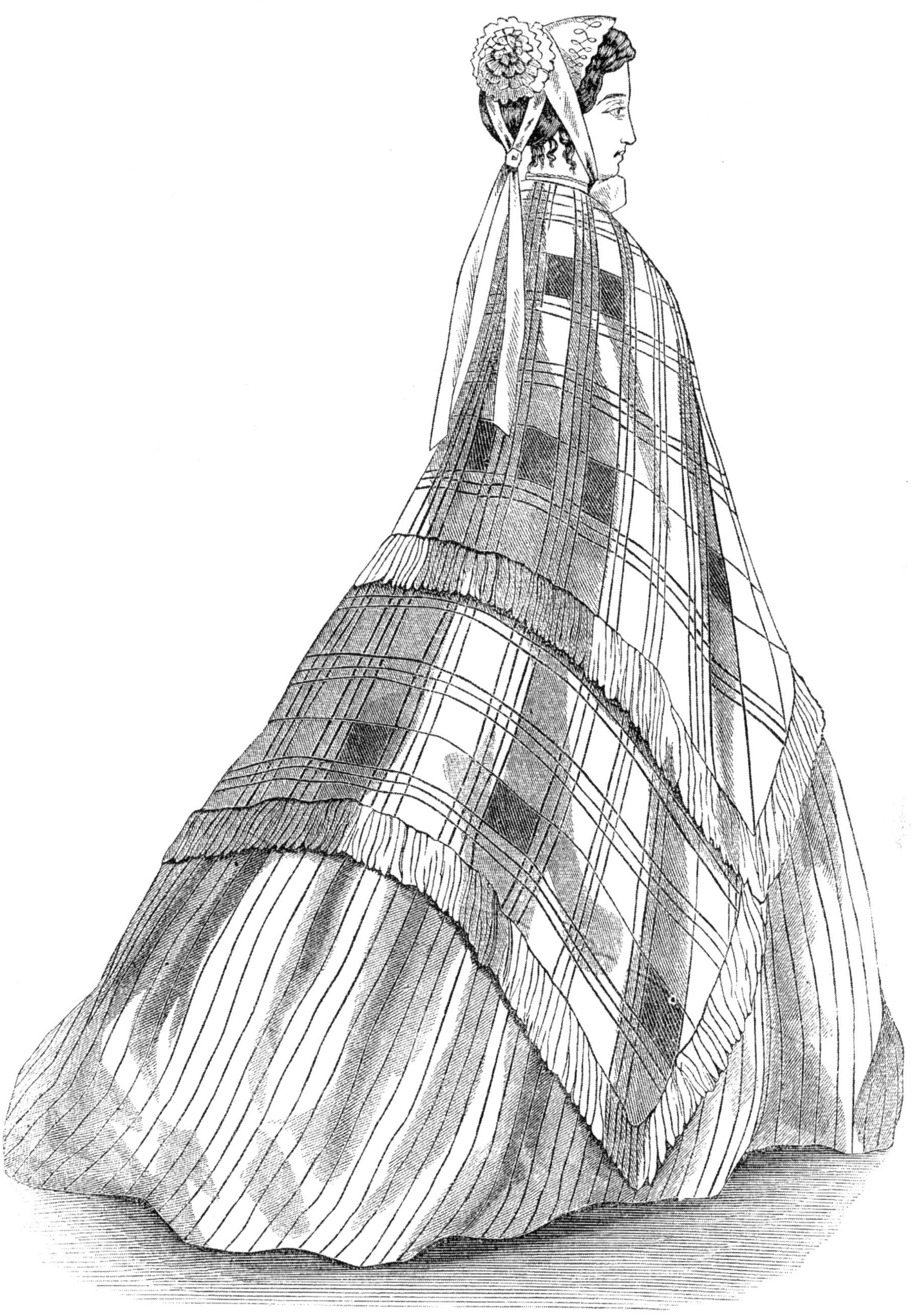

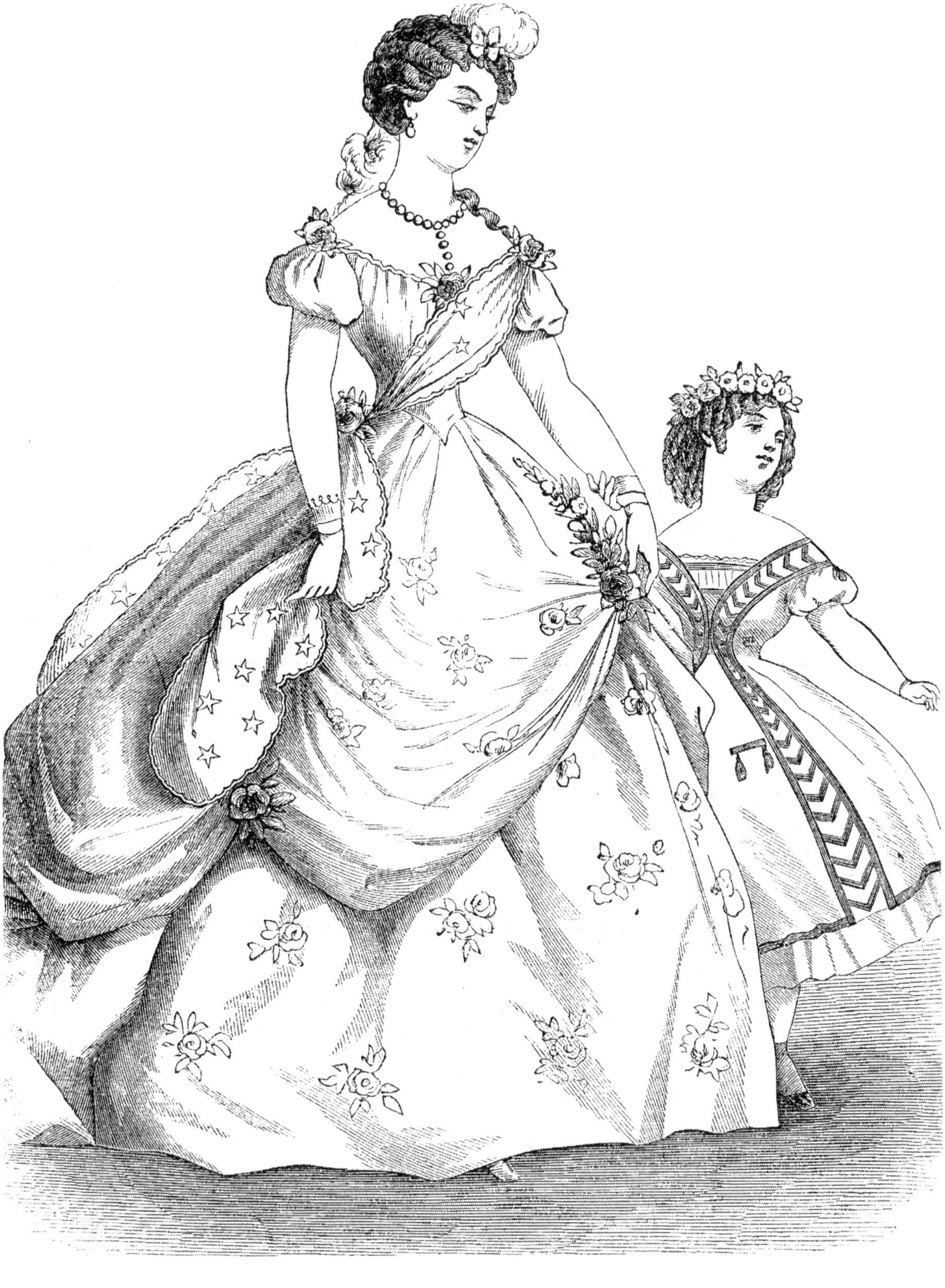

LAUDERBACH SC.

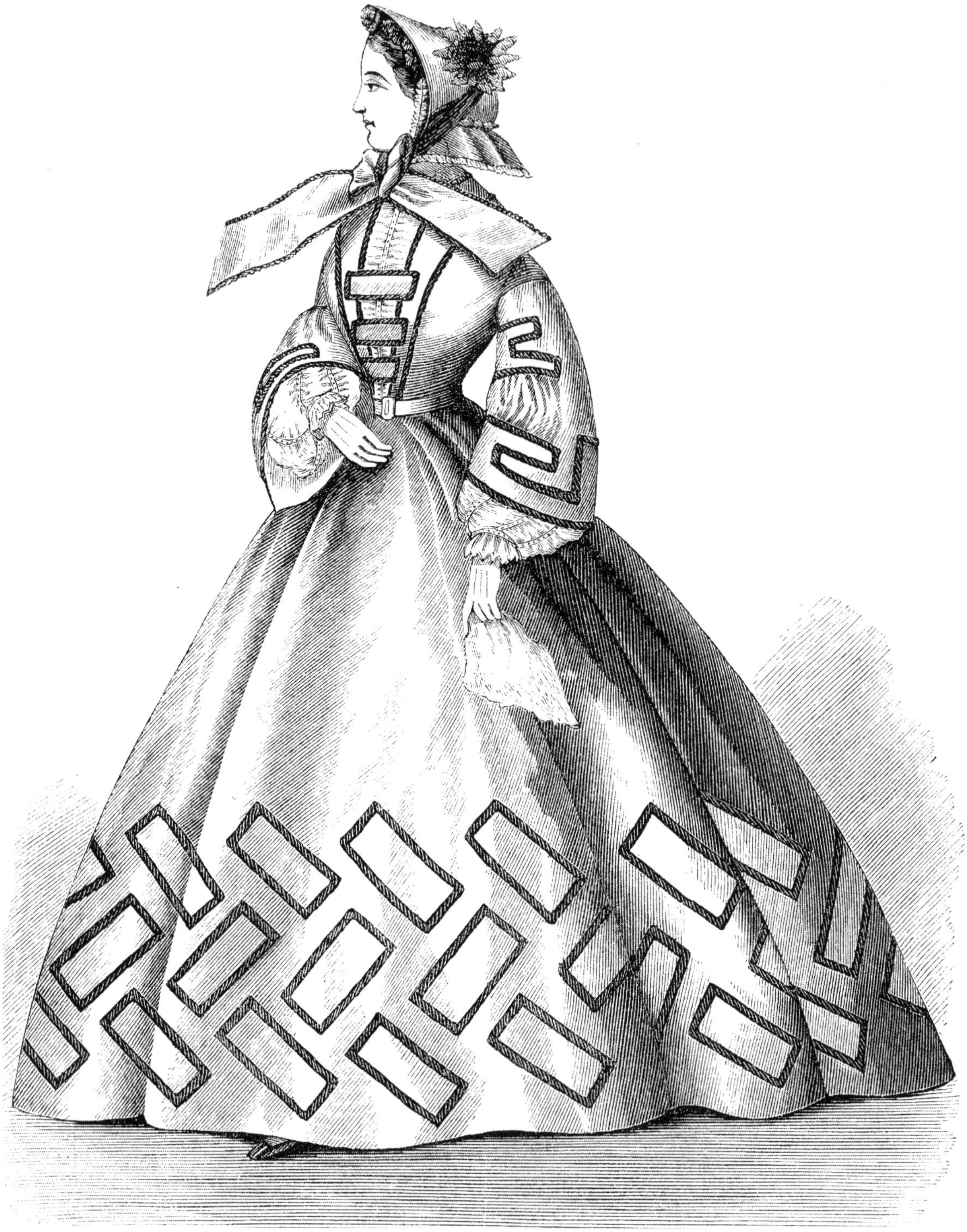

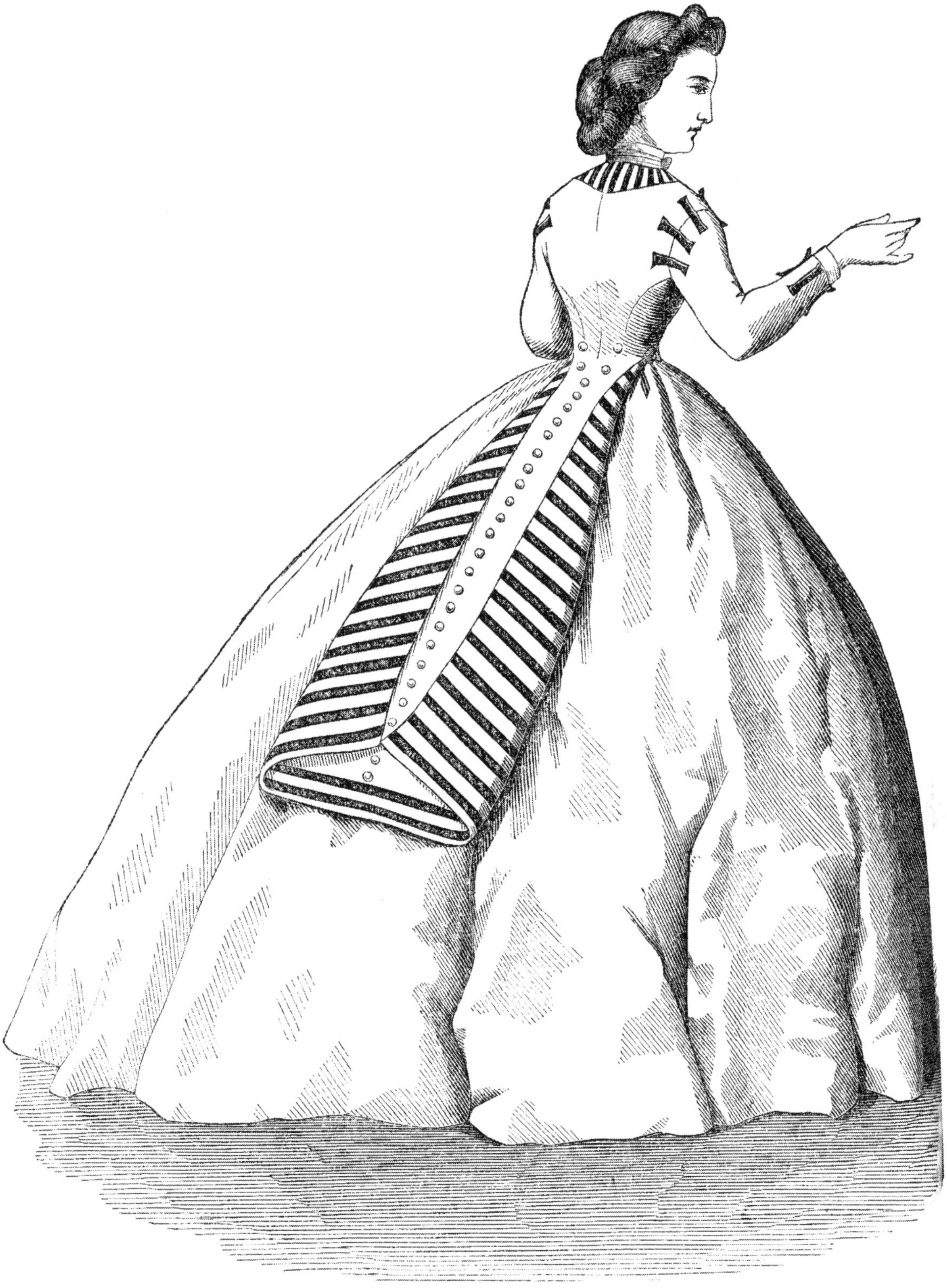

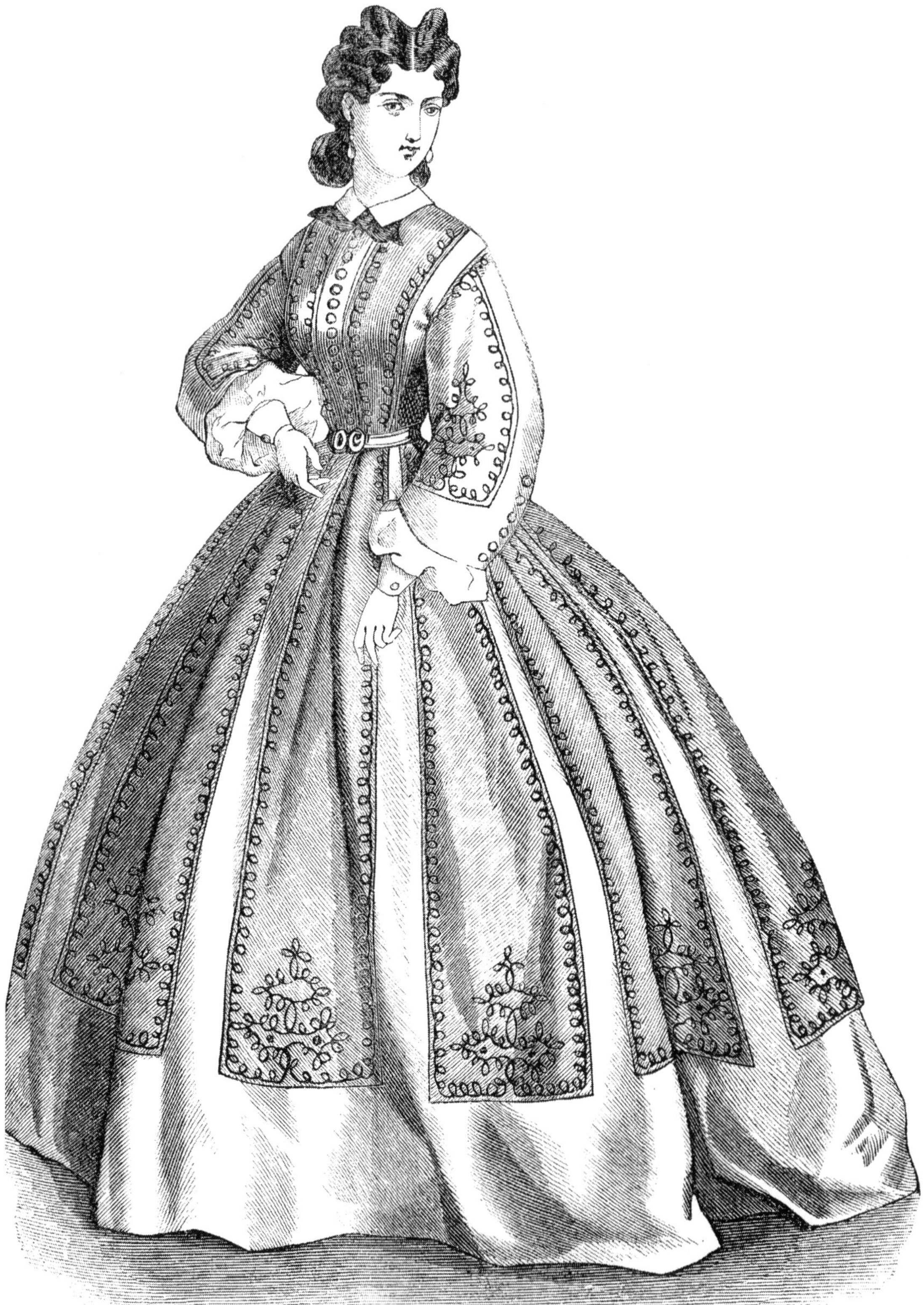

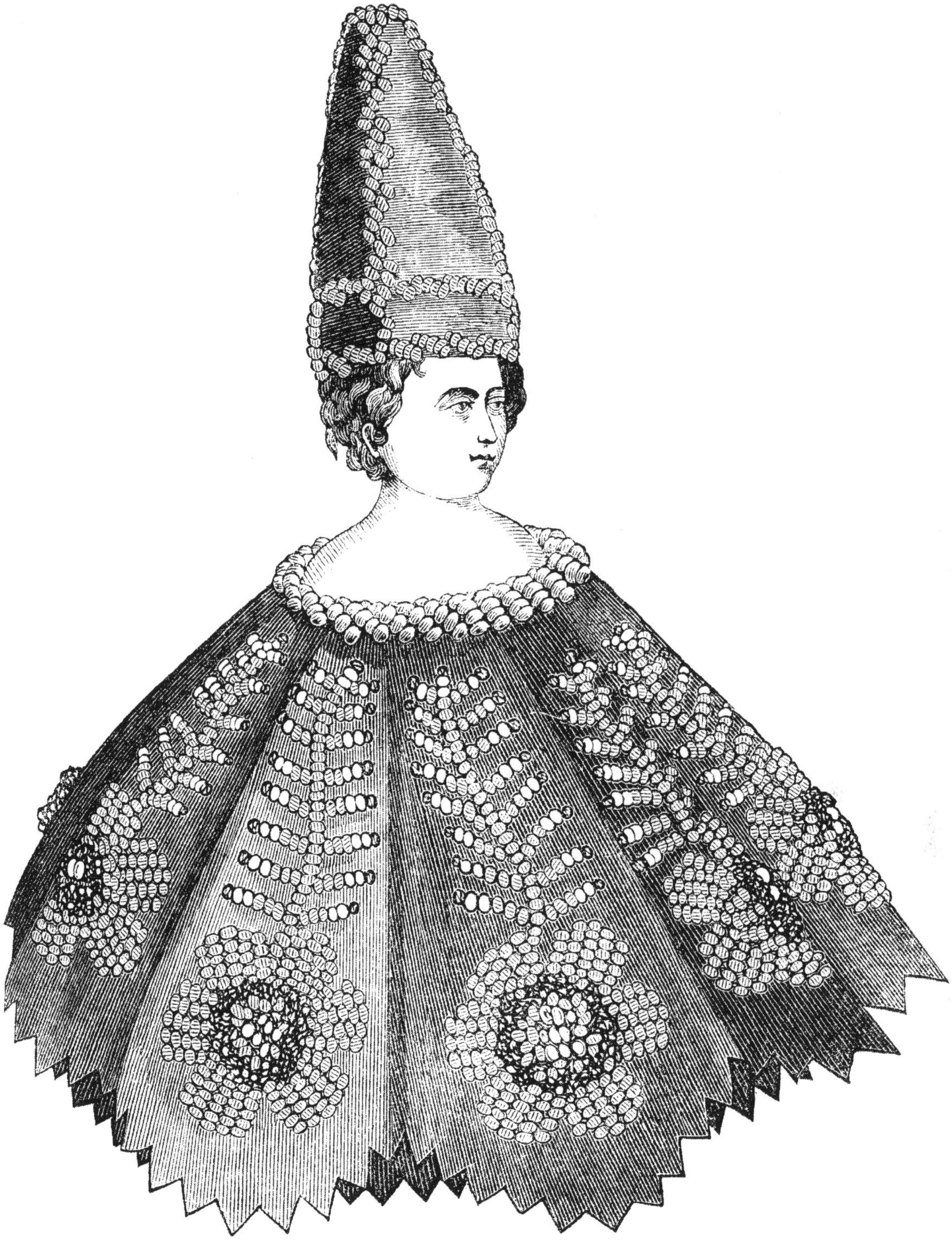

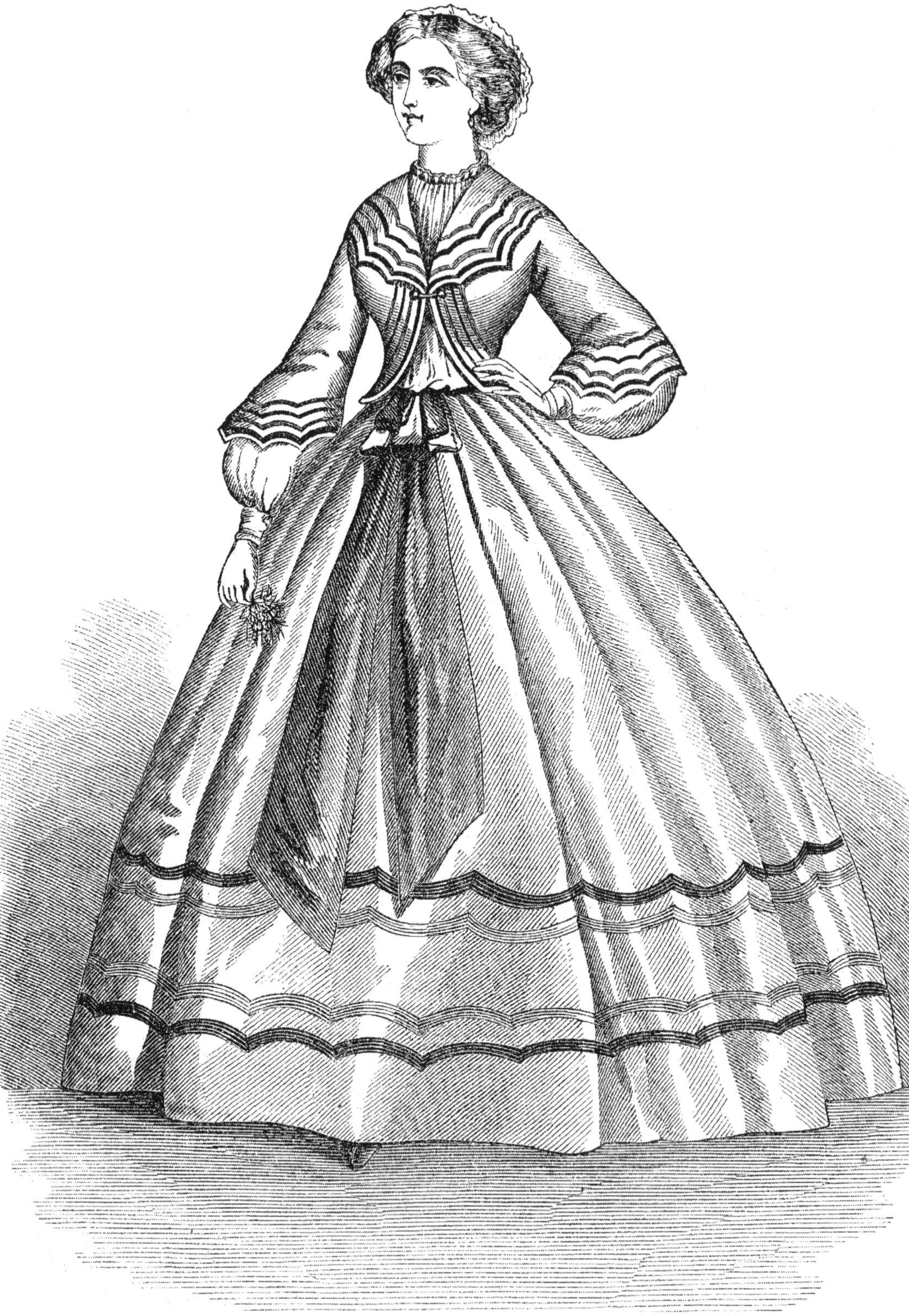

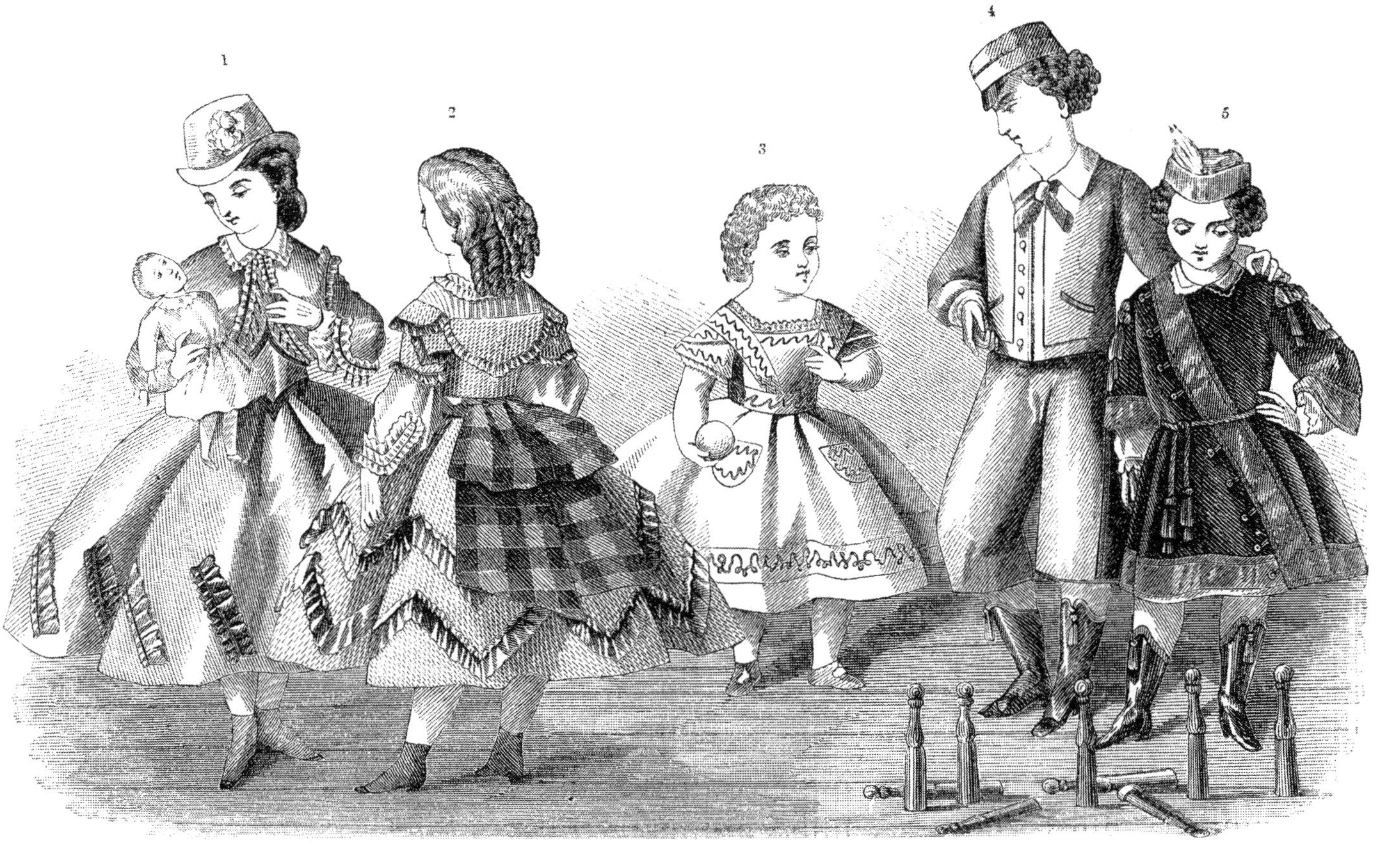
1
2
3
4
5

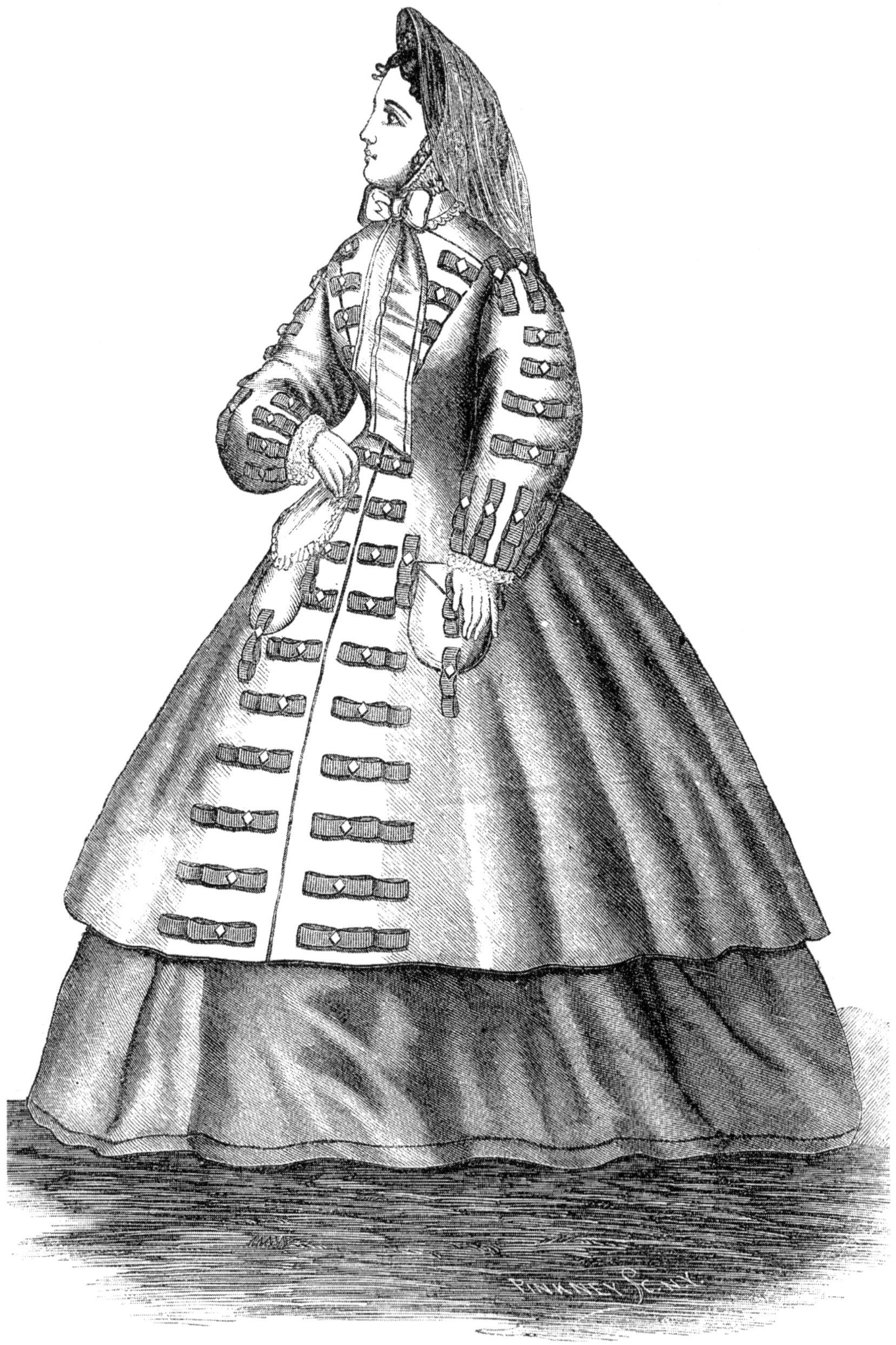
PINKNEY SC. N.Y.

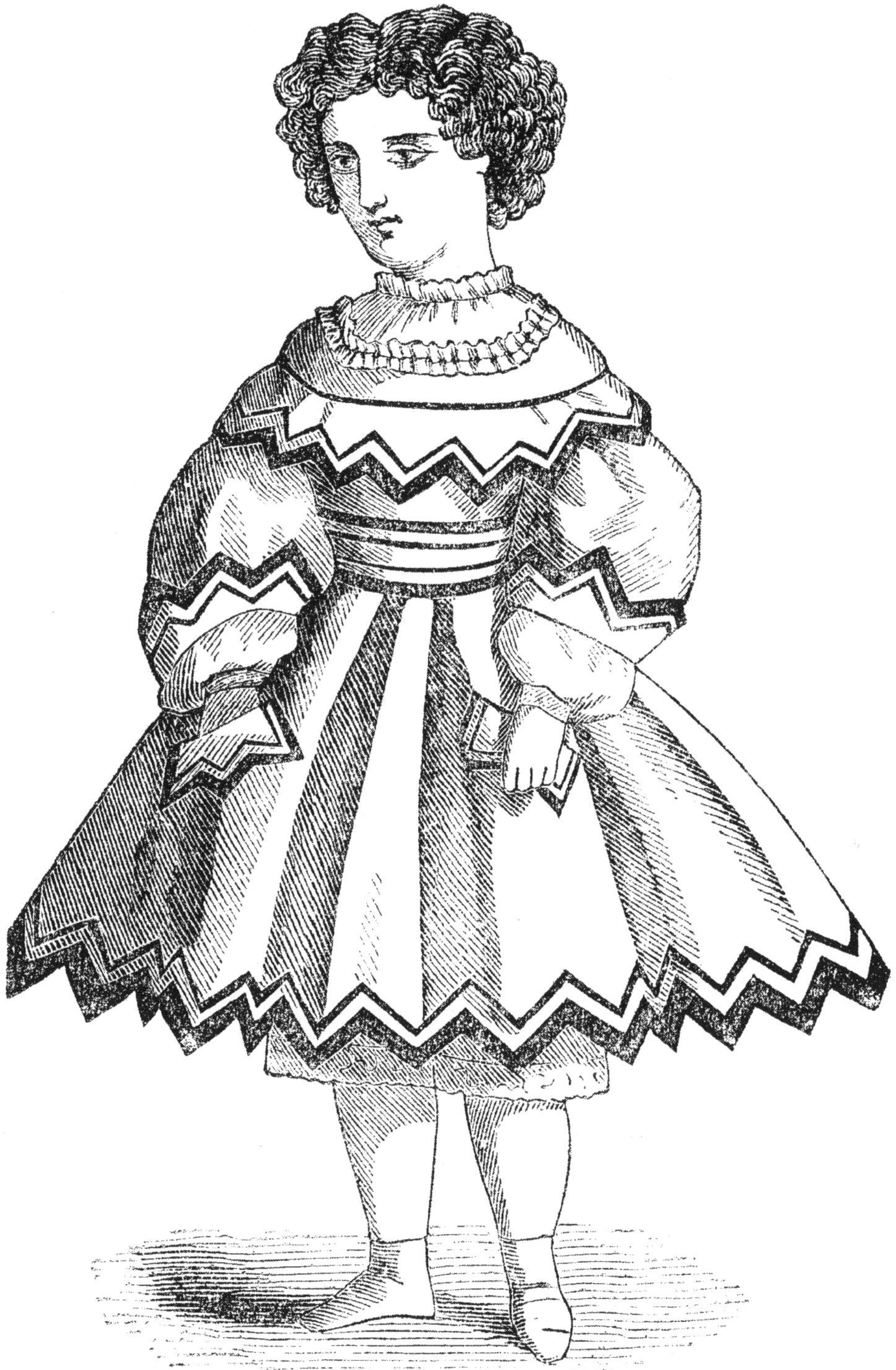

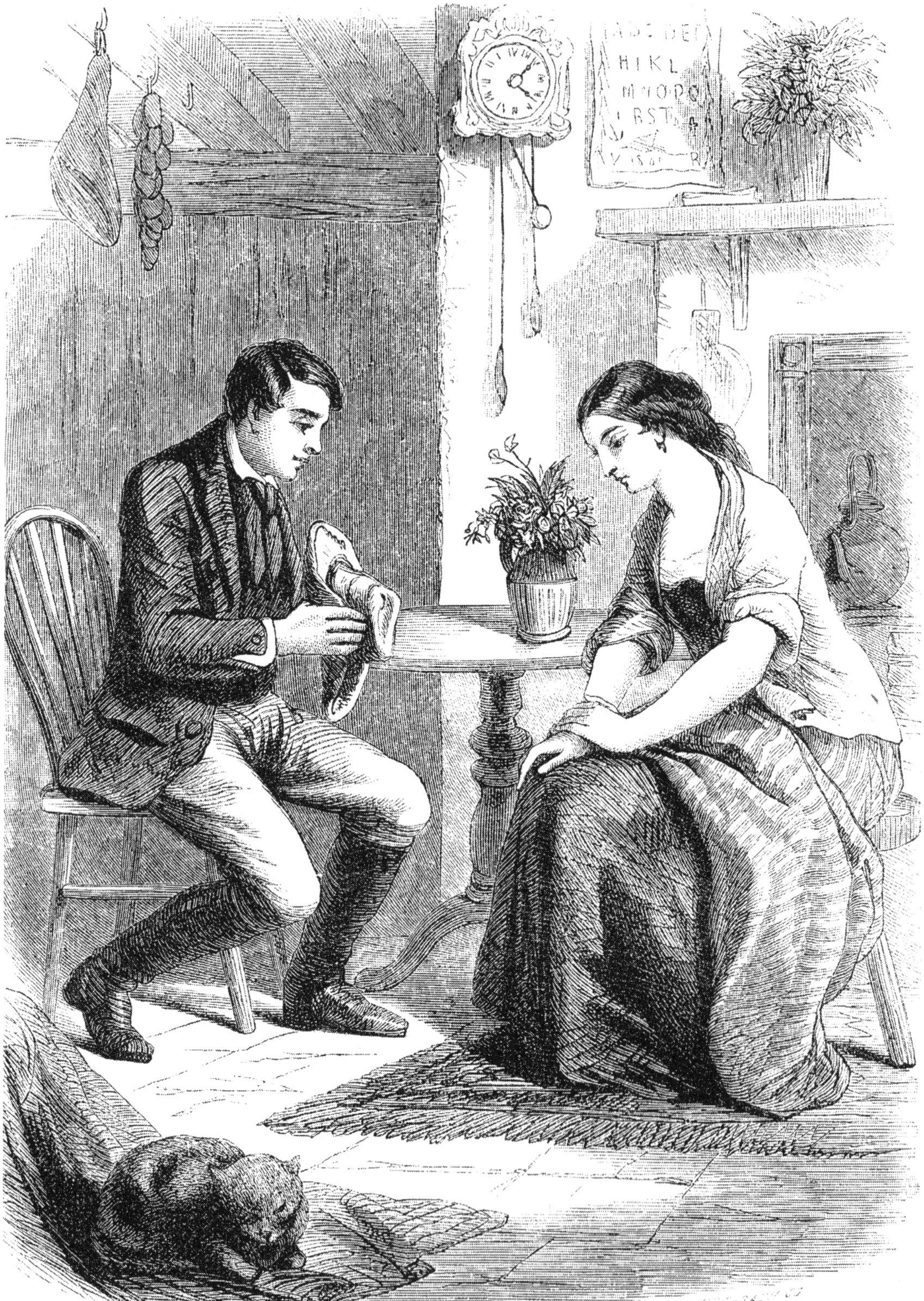

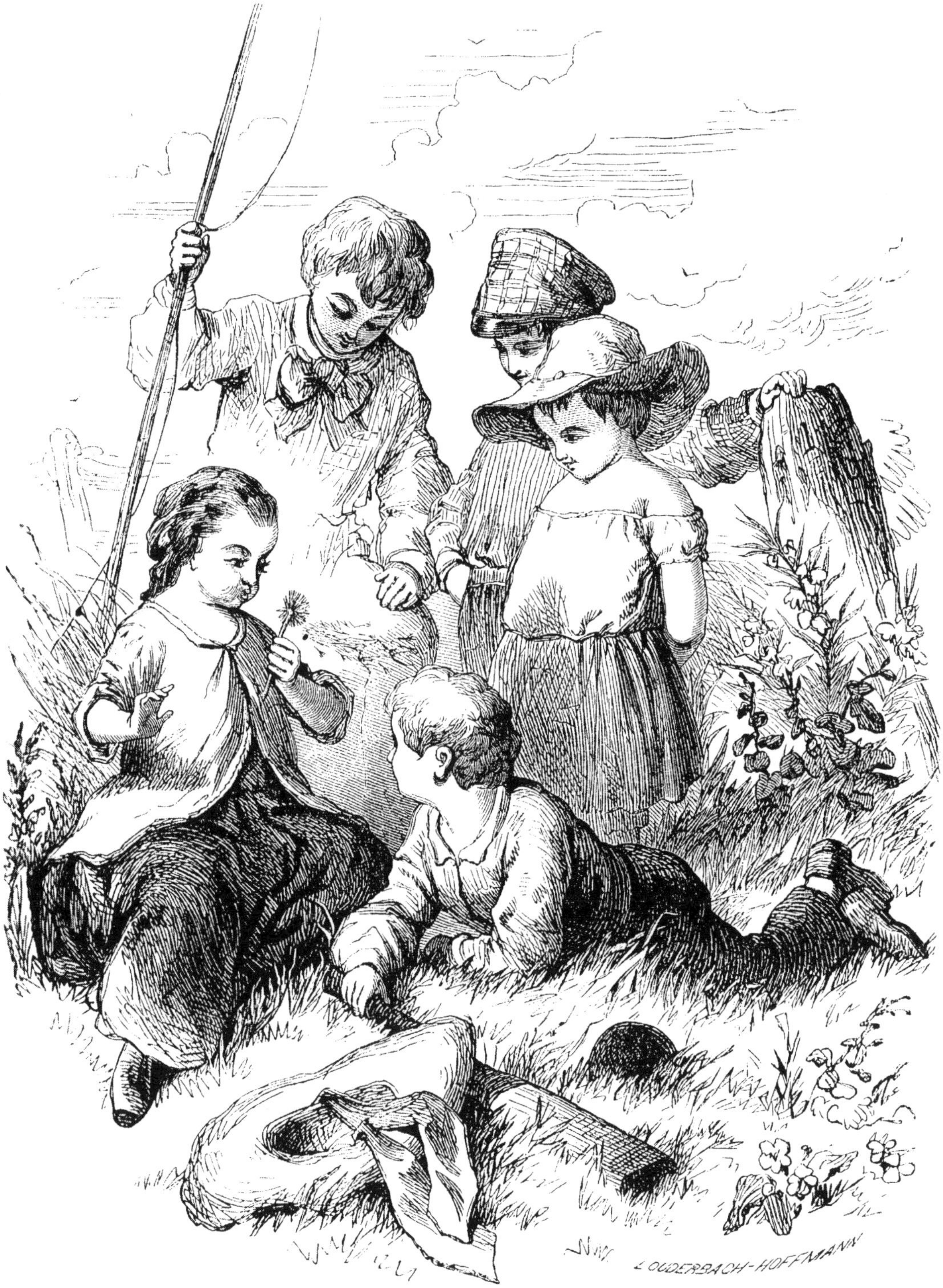
LOUDERBACH-HOFFMANN

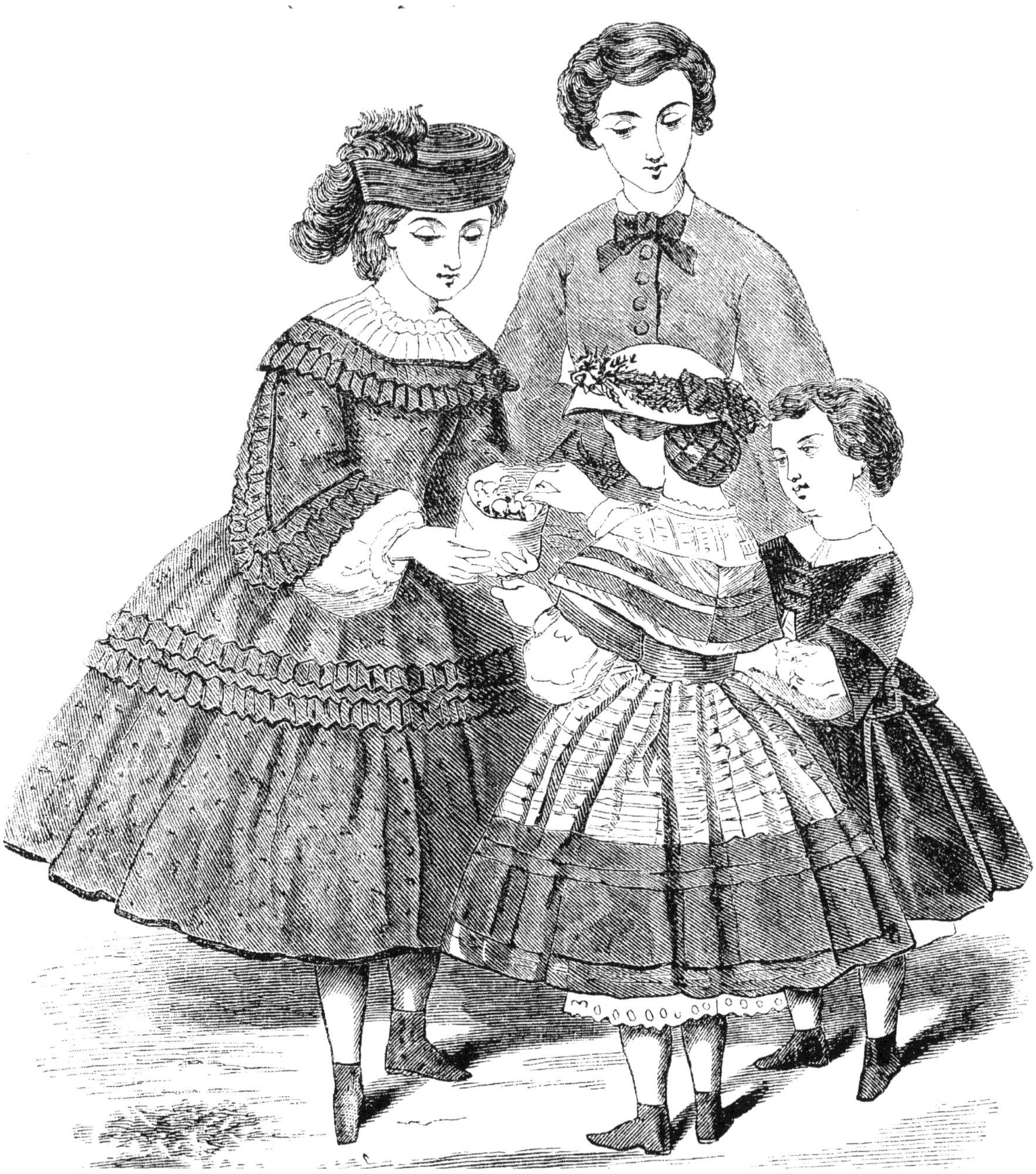

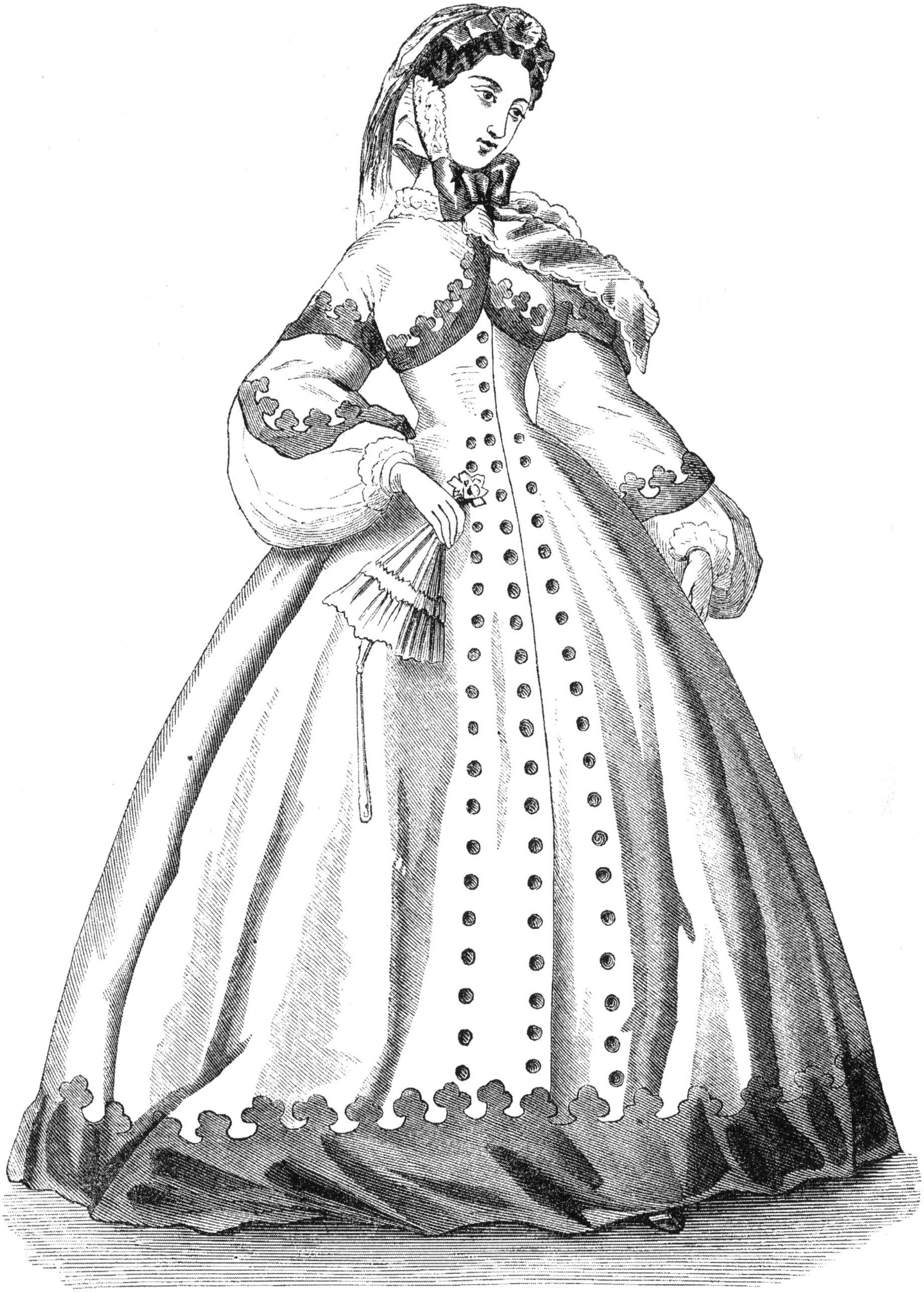

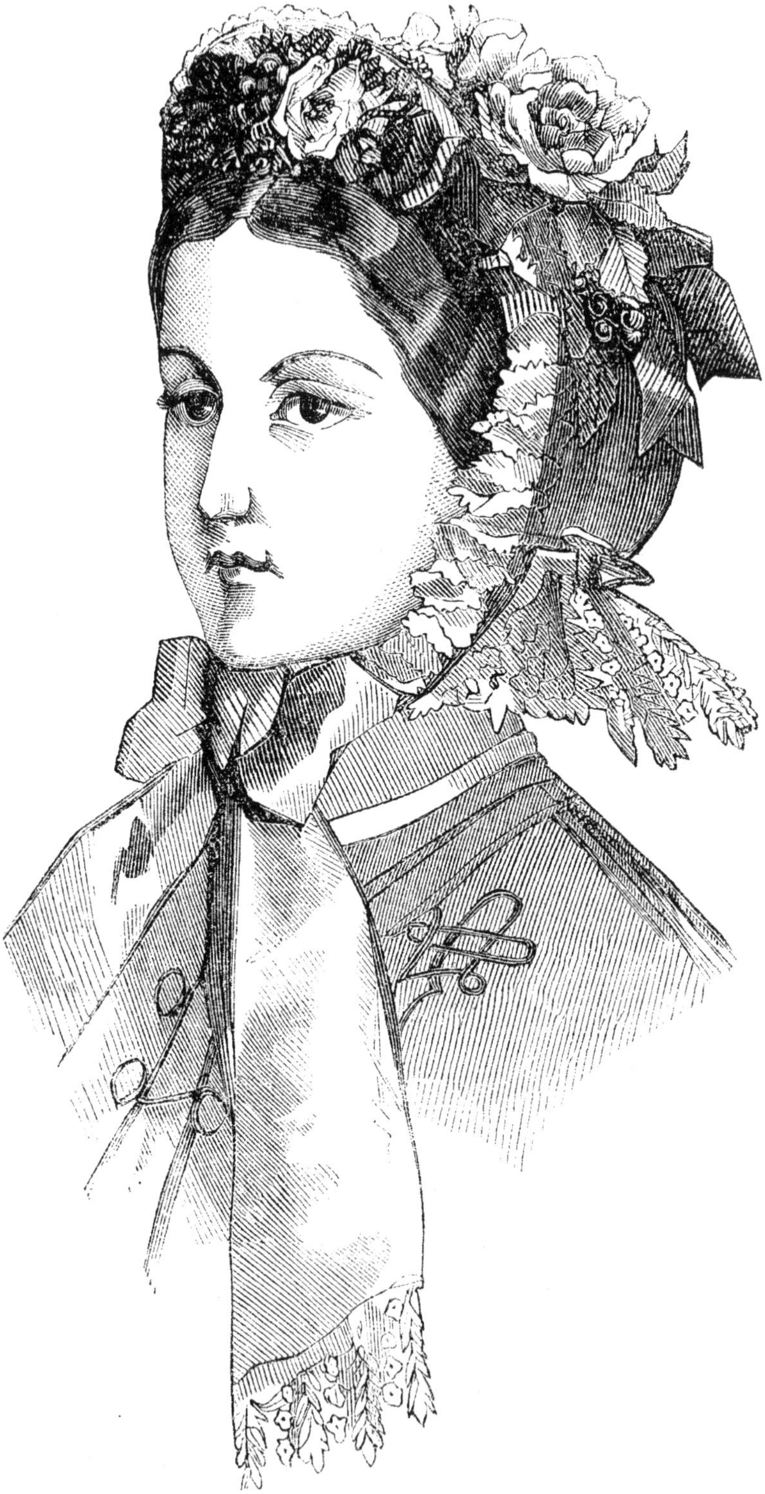

THE DOUBTFUL NOTE.

Fig. 2.   Fig 3.   Fig. 4.

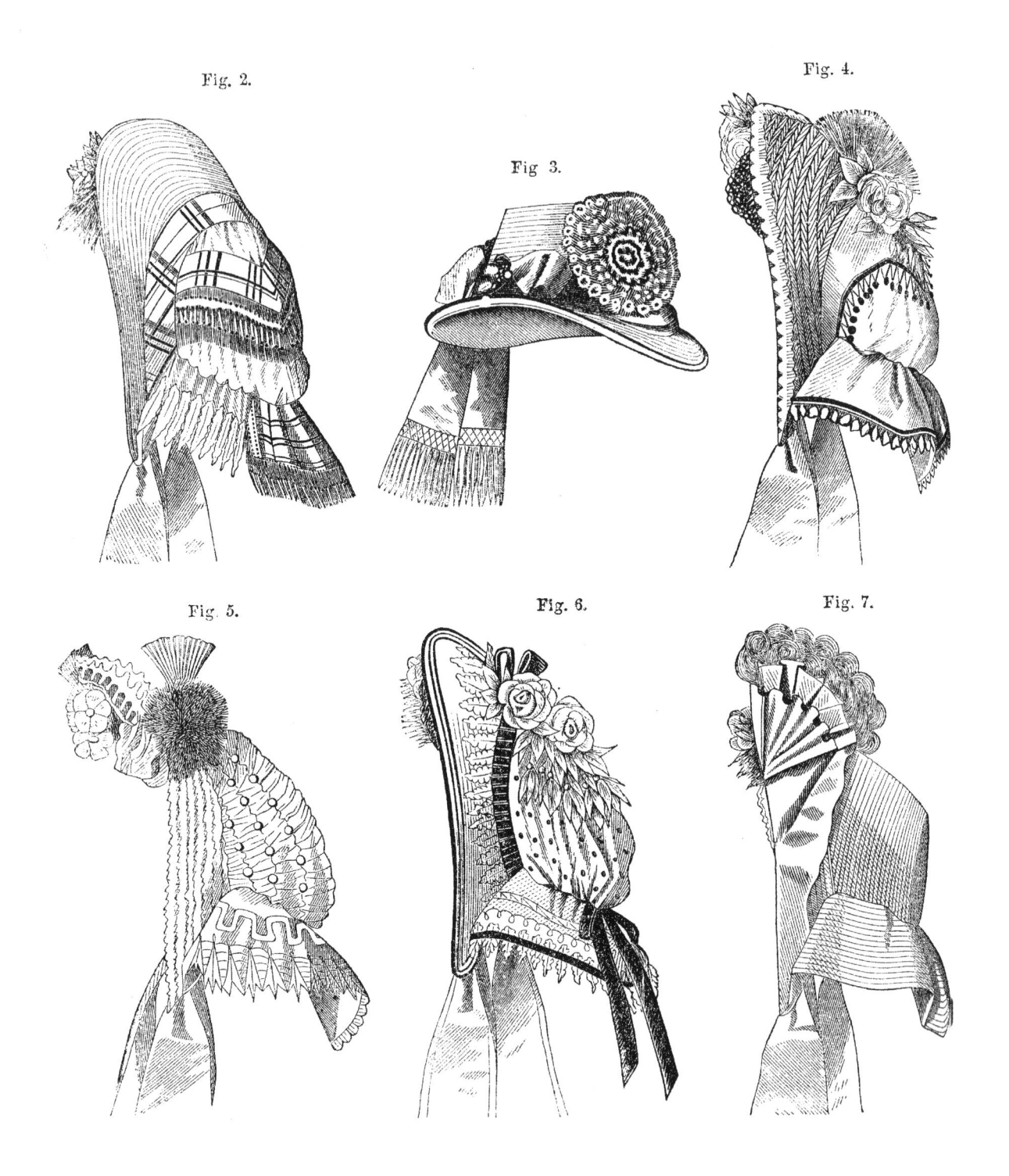

Fig. 5.   Fig. 6.   Fig. 7.

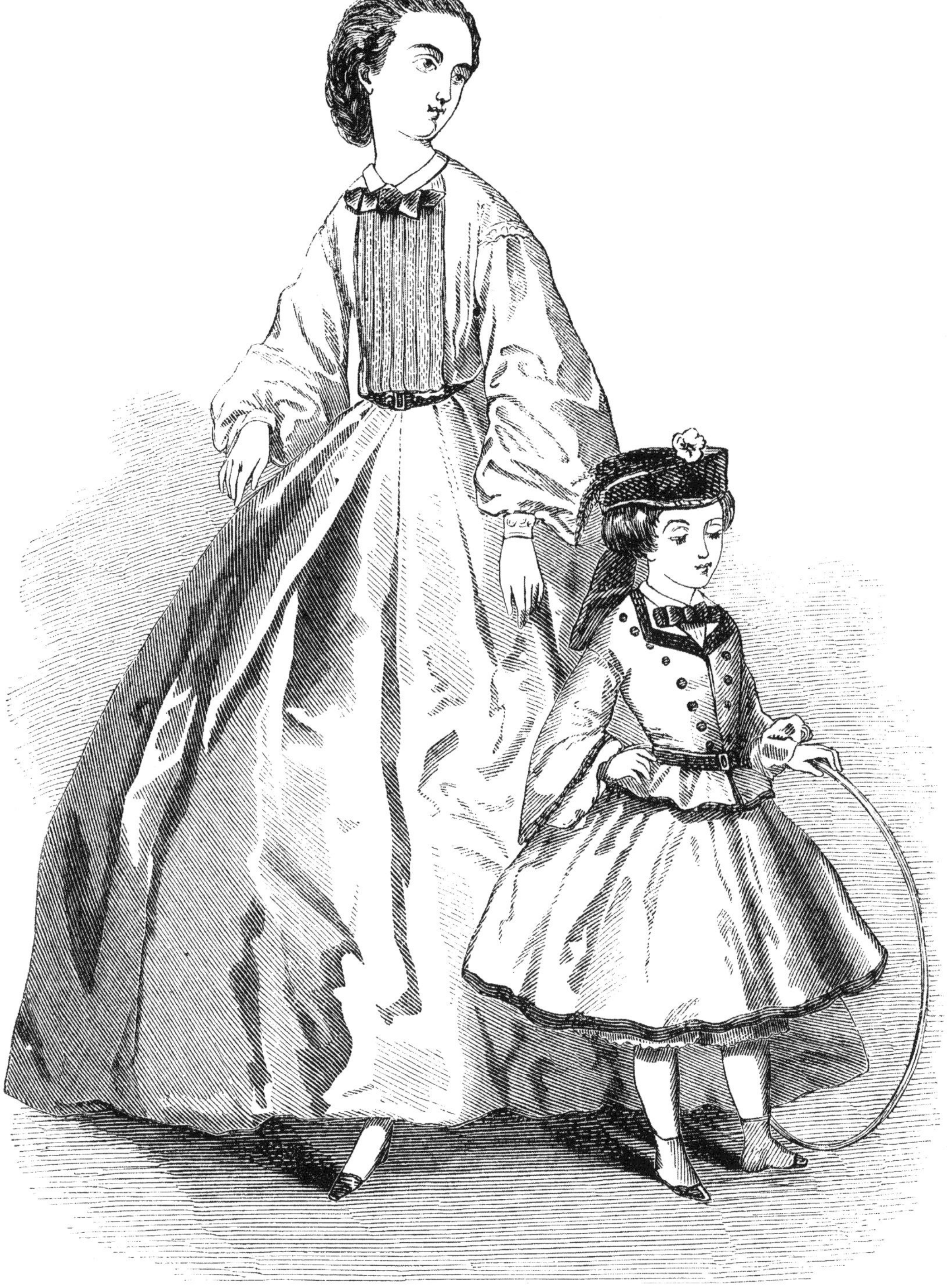

Made in the USA
Columbia, SC
30 November 2024